Coll

MAKING IT

MOVE!

A SHORT HISTORY OF ANIMATION

SAMUEL CONNOR

Contents

Have you ever wondered how a cartoon is made? Or maybe how films like *Avatar* look so realistic?

For years, a group of people have been working to bring things to life.

Who are they?

Animators!

This book is going to show you how different types of animation are made. You'll see how animators have moved from the sketchbook to the computer.

You'll even find out how to make your own animations.

How did it all start?

To make pictures "move", you need two things.

First, you need a series of drawings or photos. To show a person walking, each image would have their legs in a slightly different position.

Second, you need a way of showing these pictures quickly one after another, so it looks like the picture has come alive!

Long before film, there were clever toys that did this. One used a spinning drum with pictures on the inside.

Flip books were also popular. The viewer flicked the pages to make the picture move.

Then, in 1882, a man called Edward Muybridge made the first moving picture, using photos of a racing horse and a player called the **zoopraxiscope**. Film and animation were born!

Sticky note stick man!

To make a flip-book animation of your own, follow these simple steps:

1 Collect your materials:

- a pencil

- a pen

- a pack of sticky notes.

2 Draw a stick man on the first sticky note on the right side of the paper.

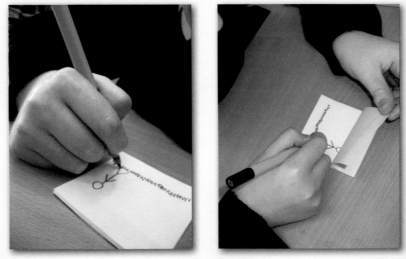

3 Turn to the next sticky note and draw him again, only moved along a little and with his arms raised a bit higher.

4 Repeat this eight more times. Each time, move the stick man across the page and raise his arms a bit further.

5 Flip through the book, and your stick man should walk and wave!

The first animations were drawn by hand. Artists had to sketch the same scenes and characters over and over. They made tiny changes in each picture or **frame**.

When the images were played quickly, one after another, it looked as if the characters were moving.

Have you seen this little black cat before?

Felix the Cat was one of the first animations
to be shown in cinemas. These cartoons were
silent and showed the adventures of a cheeky
little cat.

DID YOU KNOW?

Felix was actually called "Master Tom"
in the first cartoon he starred in. His name
was changed later.

The golden age

The 1920s and 1930s were a golden age for animation.

In 1928, Walt Disney made *Steamboat Willie*. The film starred Mickey Mouse as the captain of a riverboat. This black and white "talking picture" was one of the first animations to use sound. It was a huge hit in cinemas.

Disney and other Hollywood studios went on to make hundreds of short cartoons. Bugs Bunny first appeared in 1938. How many other cartoon stars can you name?

©Warner Bros.

Walt Disney then took a big gamble by making a full-length film. *Snow White and the Seven Dwarfs* was ten times longer than any previous cartoon. It took three years to make, and nearly broke the company. But the crowds loved it, and it went on to make a fortune at the box office.

Fact file: Walt Disney

Walt Disney was born in Chicago in 1901. He worked as a newspaper cartoonist and then he began making short cartoons to be shown in cinemas. The public loved  them, but Walt was no good with money and his first company went bust. He moved to Hollywood to try again.

Disney's big break came with his new star, Mickey Mouse.

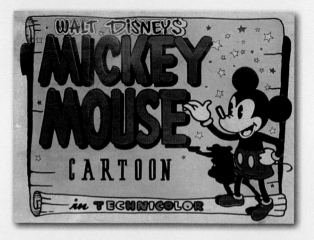

After *Steamboat Willie*, Mickey went on to appear in well over one hundred animated films. He was the first cartoon character to have a star on the Hollywood Walk of Fame.

Walt Disney studios have made many other hit films, including *Cinderella*, *Bambi* and *Peter Pan*.

Cut-out animation is one of the quickest ways of making moving pictures.

Each character and their body parts are cut out of paper. The animator does not need to keep redrawing characters, as the body parts can simply be moved around.

A camera captures each position.

The photos are then placed in order on a computer and played quickly, one after another, to create a film. This is called **stop motion**.

Charlie and Lola is a popular children's television show made using cutouts.

Do you know this man and his dog?

The *Wallace and Gromit* films are made using **claymation** (or clay animation).

The characters are made by hand, using modelling clay, plasticine or dough. Stop motion is used to take images of the characters. Tiny movements are made between each shot.

For a thirty-minute film, the animator would make over twenty thousand tiny changes, taking a photo of each change. That's slow!

Because claymation is so slow, not many blockbuster films are made this way. The animators of *Chicken Run* took six months just to make the clay characters!

An interview with Nick Park

Nick Park is the animator who made the *Wallace and Gromit* films.

Here he describes how he created Wallace and Gromit ...

When did you dream up Wallace and Gromit?

I was always sketching my own characters, ever since I was a child. I had this idea of a man who built a rocket in the basement of his house – but I wanted him to have a sidekick. That's where Gromit came in.

At first I wanted Gromit to be a cat, but a dog was easier to shape in clay. It wasn't until much later that I realised how much Wallace was based on my own Dad!

Can you tell us more about the process?

It's hard work! You tweak the clay, then you take a picture. Then you move it again and take another photo. You do that over and over again. I think one animator in a day can produce about three seconds of animation. So you need lots of animators!

I can tell when different people have worked on characters – their "take" on them somehow comes through. We have Gromit lessons for the animators who work on him. We teach them how he moves, how he looks to camera – all the things that create his personality.

Make your own claymation

Here are a few simple steps to making your own claymation.

1 Collect your materials:

- a camera

- some plasticine or clay

- a sheet of card or paper.

2 Decide on a character to bring to life – a simple ball or blob will work fine!

3 Draw a background (it could just be grass and sky).

4 Place your character in front of the background. Then take a photo.

5 Make a small change to the character. You could change its shape or move it.

6 Take another picture and repeat this until you have a series of photos.

7 Upload your images to a computer.

8 Use a program such as Windows Movie Maker to bring your animation to life.

Computer-generated animation

Computers are now at the centre of the animator's world.

But the animation still begins with a drawing, like this one from the Pixar studio.

WOODY:

BULLSEYE? ARE YOU WITH ME?

DID YOU KNOW?

Toy Story (1995) was the first film to be made in this way.

Computer animators scan in drawings and use them to create 3D digital characters. The animator first builds a **virtual skeleton** for each character.

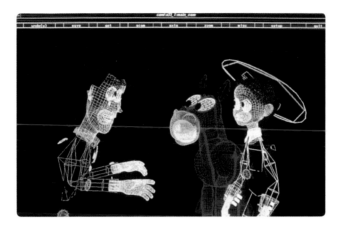

Then, he or she adds layers of colour and texture to make the characters look real.

Fact file: *Pixar*

Pixar is one of the best-known computer animation studios.

Did you know Pixar is owned by Disney?

Toy Story was Pixar's first big film. Twenty-seven animators worked on it. The character Woody was the most difficult to get right. They spent a whole week making just eight seconds of film about Woody.

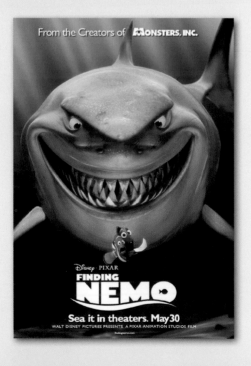

Since then, Pixar have gone on to make many more films such as *Finding Nemo* and *Cars*.

It isn't cheap to produce these kinds of animated films. It cost over one hundred and twenty million pounds to make *Toy Story 3*.

DID YOU KNOW?

The Pixar studios are so big that everyone rides around on scooters.

The animators are also given free cookies all day!

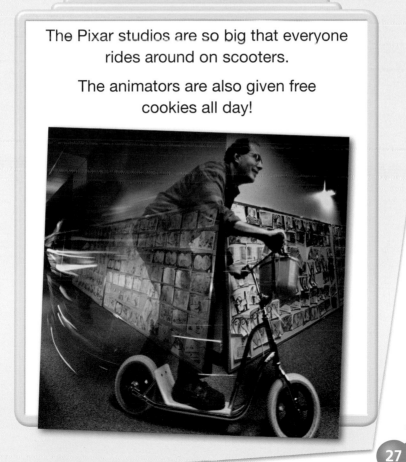

Fact file: DreamWorks

DreamWorks is another big American animation studio. They are in competition with Pixar to produce the next hit film.

Since 1994, DreamWorks have made films like *Shrek*, *Kung Fu Panda* and *How to Train your Dragon*.

To make *Kung Fu Panda*, animators spent years studying Chinese painting and buildings. This helped make the film look more realistic.

DreamWorks also make video games such as *Boom Blox* and *Medal of Honor*.

Motion capture

Have you seen the film *Avatar*? Director James Cameron had a huge team of animators to help him create his epic science fiction film. This film, with its amazing 3D graphics, broke box office records.

It was made using a method called **motion capture**. This method allowed the animators to turn real actors into strange blue creatures.

In motion capture, actors wear special suits that allow a computer to recognise them.

The animators then use special software to make them into digital characters.

DID YOU KNOW?

Avatar is set in the future on a different planet. It took the writers four years to make up a new language for the planet!

Do you play computer or video games? These also depend on animators to bring them to life.

Computer and video game animations are different from films because the gamer controls the story. The animators have to create a range of different possible endings for each game.

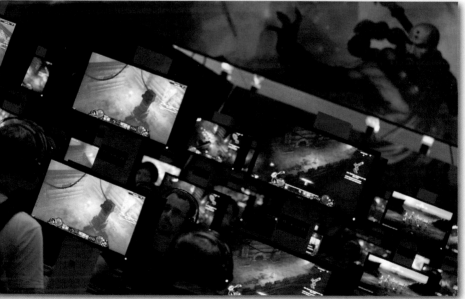

Here an animator sketches ideas by hand and uses a drawing tablet to make a new computer game.

New software applications (or 'apps') are released daily for smartphones and tablets.

There is a battle to create the top-selling app.

Lots of apps use animation to make them more exciting. For example, an animation is used to make words and letters bounce across the screen or to make an object spin when it is touched.

These apps are different from computer games because they use 2D computer animation. The animator will not need to build a virtual skeleton. They are simpler, using block colours as backgrounds.

Angry Birds *is a popular app. It's simple, but people can't stop playing it.*

One of the really exciting things about apps is that anyone can come up with an idea for one.

Many top-selling apps have been built by young people.

If you know what smartphones can do, maybe you can come up with your own idea.

12 year old Thomas Suarez is given an award for his app, Bustin Jieber.

Go create ... go animate!

There is so much more to animation than meets the eye.

With faster computers and clever software, there is no limit. More 3D animated films will be made, with even more special effects.

Maybe one day you will work for Pixar or DreamWorks, or even set up an animation studio of your own ...

"That's all folks!"

Reader challenge

Word hunt

 On page 8, find an adjective that means "very small".

 On page 11, find a word that means "risk".

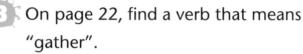 On page 22, find a verb that means "gather".

Text sense

 How many animators worked on *Toy Story*? (page 26)

 Name three films that DreamWorks have made. (page 28)

 How does the motion capture method work? (page 30–31)

 In what ways are apps different from computer games? (page 35)

Your views

8. What skills do you think you would need to be an animator?

9. Which parts of *Making it Move* did you enjoy reading? Give reasons.

Spell it

With a partner, look at these words and then cover them up.

- move
- make
- take
- moving
- making
- taking

Take it in turns for one of you to read the words aloud. The other person has to try and spell each word. Check your answers, then swap over.

Try it

With a partner, re-read pages 6 and 7. You should each make a flip-book animation of your own. Decide whose book works the best.

William Collins's dream of knowledge for all began with the publication of his first book in 1819. A self-educated mill worker, he not only enriched millions of lives, but also founded a flourishing publishing house. Today, staying true to this spirit, Collins books are packed with inspiration, innovation and practical expertise. They place you at the centre of a world of possibility and give you exactly what you need to explore it.

Collins. Freedom to teach.

Published by Collins Education
An imprint of HarperCollins*Publishers*
77–85 Fulham Palace Road, Hammersmith, London W6 8JB

Browse the complete Collins Education catalogue at **www.collinseducation.com**

Text by Sam Connor
© HarperCollins*Publishers* Limited 2012

Series consultants: Alan Gibbons and Natalie Packer

10 9 8 7 6 5 4 3 2 1
ISBN 978-0-00-748906-0

British Library Cataloguing in Publication Data.
A catalogue record for this publication is available from the British Library.

Commissioned by Catherine Martin

Edited and project-managed by Sue Chapple

Picture research and proofreading by Grace Glendinning

Design and typesetting by Jordan Publishing Design Limited

Cover design by Paul Manning

Acknowledgements

The publishers would like to thank the students and teachers of the following schools for their help in trialling the Read On series:

Langham C of E Primary School, Langham, Rutland
Ratton School, Eastbourne, East Sussex
Northfleet School for Girls, North Fleet, Kent
Westergate Community School, Chichester, West Sussex
Bottesford C of E Primary School, Bottesford, Nottinghamshire
Woodfield Academy, Redditch, Worcestershire
St Richard's Catholic College, Bexhill, East Sussex

The publishers gratefully acknowledge the permission granted to reproduce the copyright material in this book. While every effort has been made to trace and contact copyright holders, where this has not been possible the publishers will be pleased to make the necessary arrangements at the first opportunity.

The publisher would like to thank the following for permission to reproduce pictures in these pages (t = top, b = bottom, c = centre, l = left, r = right):

Images and interview on pp 16–21 used with permission from Aardman Animations Ltd., Bristol.
pp 2 & 30 TM & © 20th Century Fox/Everett/Rex Features, p 3 Jeff Morgan 03/Alamy, p 4 SSPL/Getty Images, p 5 Muybridge, Eadweard, 1830-1904/Library of Congress, p 8 Movie:CHER AMI (2009), Company: ACCIÓ (infinit Animacions S.L.), Director: Miquel Pujol, Animation Artist: Pablo Navarro, Animation Director-Character Animator, p 9 Image courtesy of Don Oriolo and Felix the Cat Creations, Inc. All rights reserved TM & © 2012 FTCP, Inc., p 10b Pictorial Press Ltd/Alamy, p 10t & 11 SNAP/Rex Features, p 12t Mondadori via Getty Images, p 12b Everett Collection/Rex Features, p 13 © W.Disney/Everett/Rex Features, p 14 Art and animation by Luca Dipierro, from film entitled ACROBATI (video, 2012), p 15 Image of Charlie and Lola from Lauren Child's *I Am Too Absolutely Small for School* published by and provided courtesy of Orchard Books and used with permission from David Higham Associates, p 16, 17, 20, 29 & 30r AF archive/Alamy, p 18 ITV/Rex Features, p 21 © Aardman Animations 2009, p 24, 25b, 25t & 26 Moviestore collection Ltd/Alamy, p 27 Science Faction/SuperStock, p 30l TM & copyright 20th Century Fox/Everett/Rex Features, p 31 Melanie Stetson Freeman/The Christian Science Monitor via Getty Images, p 32 OLIVER BERG/AFP/Getty Images, p 33 Picture Contact BV/Alamy, p 34 Urbanmyth/Alamy, p 35 Vinod Kurien/Alamy, p 36 Jemal Countess/Getty Images, p 37 Pictorial Press Ltd/Alamy.

Front cover: Computer game animator at work © Picture Contact BV/Alamy
Back cover: Comic book art, mishkom/iStock photo